Brands We Know

Parker Brothers

By Sara Green

Bellwether Media • Minneapolis, MN

Jump into the cockpit and take flight with Pilot books. Your journey will take you on high-energy adventures as you learn about all that is wild, fascinating, and fun!

This edition first published in 2018 by Bellwether Media, Inc.

Library of Congress Cataloging-in-Publication Data

Names: Green, Sara, 1964- author.
Title: Parker Brothers / by Sara Green.
Description: Minneapolis, MN : Bellwether Media, Inc., [2018] | Series: Pilot: Brands We Know | Includes bibliographical references and index. | Audience: Grades 3-8
Identifiers: LCCN 2016055078 (print) | LCCN 2017014634 (ebook) | ISBN 9781626176546 (hardcover : alk. paper) | 9781681033846 (ebook)
Subjects: LCSH: Parker Brothers, inc.--History--Juvenile literature. | Board games--United States--History--Juvenile literature. | Board game industry--United States--History--Juvenile literature.
Classification: LCC HD9993.G354 (ebook) | LCC HD9993.G354 P3747 2018 (print) | DDC 338.7/617940973--dc23
LC record available at https://lccn.loc.gov/2016055078

Editor: Betsy Rathburn   Designer: Josh Brink

Printed in the United States of America, North Mankato, MN.

PARKER BROTHERS

Table of Contents

What Is Parker Brothers?

It is family game night! Board games line the shelves of a cabinet. Favorites include *Monopoly, Clue*, and *Trivial Pursuit*. These games all have something in common. Each was once a Parker Brothers game! Which game will the family choose? Tonight, they agree on *Clue*. Next time, another game will come out of the cabinet!

Parker Brothers is a toy and game **brand** owned by Hasbro, Inc. Hasbro is one of the largest toy companies on Earth. Company **headquarters** is in Pawtucket, Rhode Island. Between 1883 and 1991, Parker Brothers made more than 1,800 games. They included *Sorry!, Pit,* and *Rook*. These games are still played by people all over the world. *Monopoly, Clue*, and *Trivial Pursuit* are among the top-selling board games of all time!

Classic Detective Game

1980s-2000s *Clue* **tagline**

Clue

By the Numbers

more than
55 million
Rook decks sold since 1906

more than
300
versions of *Monopoly* made

10
rooms in original *Clue* game mansion

Clue sold in more than
40
countries

more than
50
different *Trivial Pursuit* editions sold

around
1 billion
Monopoly players over time

$20,580
of *Monopoly* money in every game

Hasbro headquarters in Pawtucket, Rhode Island

A Game Inventor

George S. Parker was born in Salem, Massachusetts, in 1866. He had two older brothers named Charles and Edward. As a teenager, George enjoyed playing games with his friends. One was a card game called *Everlasting*. But George grew bored with the game. He added new cards and changed the rules. This became a new game that George called *Banking*.

George's friends and family loved playing *Banking*. They believed other people would also enjoy the game. George decided to ask **publishers** to print *Banking*. He was unsuccessful, but he did not give up. He started selling the game on his own in 1883. George spent about $40 to make 500 sets of the game. He sold door-to-door to local shops. In time, he sold almost every game and earned a **profit** of around $100!

currants

A Fruitful Job
George earned the money to publish *Banking* by selling currants grown in his family's garden.

George S. Parker

**Parker Brothers...
way ahead of
the game**
1970s tagline

7

After graduating from high school, George worked as a **journalist** for a newspaper. But George missed making games. He left the newspaper in 1886 and returned to selling games. One year later, he opened a game store with his earnings. George sold games both he and others had invented. In early 1888, George was joined by his brother Charles. Together, the two men formed Parker Brothers. George created games and Charles handled **finances**. In time, their eldest brother, Edward, also joined the company.

Ping-Pong
George discovered *Ping-Pong* in England and brought it to the United States in 1902. Many know this game as table tennis today.

Tiddledy Winks

The company's early games included *Yale-Harvard Game* and *Ye Yankee Peddler*. These games were popular in New England. But Parker Brothers wanted to make games that would appeal to more people. George began making trips to Europe in the late 1800s. There, he discovered games that Europeans enjoyed playing. One was a flicking game called *Tiddledy Winks*. Another was a balloon game called *Pillow-Dex*. George introduced them in America, where they became huge hits. Parker Brothers sales soared!

The Hits Keep Coming!

By the early 1900s, Parker Brothers was among the top game companies in the United States. In 1906, the company launched a card game called *Rook*. Eventually, it became the best-selling game in the country. Other popular Parker Brothers games at that time included *Flinch* and *Pit*. But in 1929, the **Great Depression** slowed the booming business. Many people could not afford to buy games. Parker Brothers struggled to stay in business. It needed another best seller to stay afloat.

Rook

Own It All

2000s *Monopoly* tagline

Winning Big

Every few years, top players from around the world compete in the *Monopoly* World Championship. The grand prize is $20,580. This is the total amount of money in a *Monopoly* set!

2009 *Monopoly* World Championship

In 1935, Parker Brothers introduced a board game called *Monopoly*. The game let players earn pretend money by trading properties. People loved *Monopoly*. Soon, the company was making thousands of sets each week. Parker Brothers was back on track!

About a decade later, a British board game called *Cluedo* led to another Parker Brothers hit. Players had to find clues to solve a murder in a mansion. The company got the **rights** to sell the game in 1949 and renamed it *Clue*.

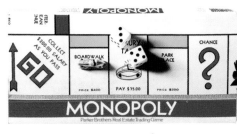

Monopoly

George Parker died in 1952 at the age of 86. Although the company had lost its founder, Parker Brothers continued making games. The **strategy** board game *Risk* **debuted** in the United States in 1959. To play, players rolled dice to take over the world. Over time, many more versions of *Risk* have been made. They include *Risk Europe, Risk Star Trek,* and *Risk Star Wars*. The new boards may look different, but the **object** stays the same!

Parker Brothers' success continued into the 1960s and 1970s. Parker Brothers released a board game called *Ouija* in 1967. Players used it to find answers to their questions. More than two million boards were sold that year.

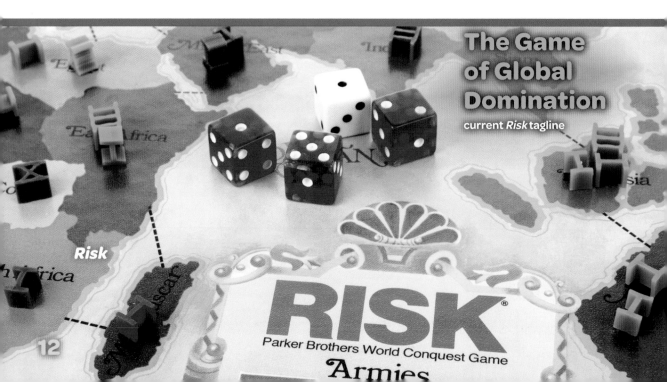

The Game
of Global
Domination

current *Risk* tagline

Risk

RISK®

Parker Brothers World Conquest Game

Armies

Nerf blasters

In 1970, the company introduced a foam ball called the Nerf ball. It was an instant success! The Nerf line grew quickly. Popular toys included footballs and basketballs. Over time, blasters and other Nerf weapons became top sellers.

Nerf footballs

Nerf ball

Changes And Growth

In the late 1970s, Parker Brothers began making handheld games with electronic parts. The first one, a game called *Code Name: Sector*, did not sell well. However, the company released a new electronic game called *Merlin* in 1978. It became a best seller! Parker Brothers entered the video game market in the 1980s. *Frogger* and *Star Wars: The Empire Strikes Back* were among its most successful games. Meanwhile, the ownership of Parker Brothers changed twice. In 1985, the company joined Kenner to become Kenner Parker Toys. Two years later, it joined another large toy company called Tonka.

The growing company made an important move in 1989. It bought the rights to a hit board game called *Trivial Pursuit*. This game tested what players knew about different topics. Over time, the number of copies sold has topped 100 million. It is one of the best-selling games in history!

Merlin

Frogger

Popular Parker Brothers Games

Pit

Sorry!

Rook

Risk

Payday

Masterpiece

Game	Year
Pit	1903
Flinch	1905
Rook	1906
Sorry!	1934
Monopoly	1935
Clue	1949
Risk	1959
Ouija	1966
Masterpiece	1970
Boggle	1972
Payday	1975
Merlin	1978
Star Wars: The Empire Strikes Back	1982
Trivial Pursuit	1989

Memory Challenges

The original *Trivial Pursuit* had 6,000 questions and 1,000 cards. Over time, more than 50 special editions have been made. They include *Trivial Pursuit for Kids* and *Pop Culture*.

A large toy company called Hasbro, Inc. bought Parker Brothers in 1991. Today, the Parker Brothers **logo** no longer appears on its toys and games. But playing with them is still as fun as ever! Both kids and adults enjoy battles with Nerf weapons. Family and friends gather to play *Sorry!* or *Risk*.

Handle With Care

The most expensive *Monopoly* set in the world is valued at $2 million. It is made of gold and gemstones. The dice alone are worth $10,000!

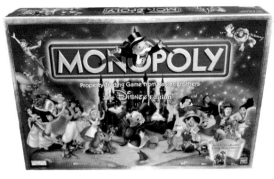

2017 Monopoly tokens

Disney Monopoly

Over the years, the company has made changes to give games a more modern look. In *Clue*, the mansion now has a movie theater and a spa. A scientist named Dr. Orchid replaced Mrs. White, a housekeeper. The company has made *Monopoly* more modern, too. In 2017, a T. rex, a rubber duck, and a penguin replaced three original game **tokens**. Hasbro has also created new versions of the game such as *Nintendo Monopoly* and *Disney Monopoly*. There is even a *Monopoly* **app**. People can download it to their mobile devices. Now they can play the classic board game anytime, anywhere!

Clue mansion

DR. ORCHID

More Places To Play

Parker Brothers toys and games help make a difference. In 2005, Hasbro launched the Tonka Truck Tour. A life-size Tonka truck visited 14 states to collect toys for victims of Hurricane Katrina. Each year, the Hasbro Children's Hospital in Rhode Island holds a toy-themed **charity** event. In 2014, the *Monopoly* Ball raised more than $1 million! More than 1,000 people attended this event. Guests could be the first to buy special Rhode Island-themed *Monopoly* games. The money made from sales of the games went to the hospital.

Nerf Energy game kits help kids stay active and healthy. The kits include an activity tracker, a Nerf soccer ball, and an app game called *Energy Rush*. As kids move, they earn points to play the game! Nerf helps in other ways, too. In 2016, the world's largest Nerf battle took place in Arlington, Texas. More than 2,200 people used 4,394 blasters to fight for victory and raise money for charity. Parker Brothers toys and games add fun to people's lives!

tonkatrucktour.com

Hasbro Tonka Truck Tour

Tonka TRUCK TOUR '05

19

Parker Brothers Timeline

1885
George Parker founds the
George S. Parker Company

1952
George S. Parker
passes away

1970
The company
begins selling
the Nerf ball

1898
Edward Parker
joins the company

1968
General Mills buys
Parker Brothers

1888
George and Charles
Parker start
Parker Brothers

1935
Parker Brothers
buys the rights to
Monopoly

1902
Ping-Pong is
introduced to the
United States

1973
First *Monopoly* World
Championship is held
in New York

1986

George Parker is added to the Toy Industry Hall of Fame

1991

Hasbro buys Tonka and the Parker Brothers brand

2017

Hasbro updates three of the *Monopoly* tokens

1993

Trivial Pursuit is added to the *Games* magazine Games Hall of Fame

1985

A movie based on *Clue* comes out in theaters

1999

Hasbro releases a Pokémon version of *Monopoly*

2008

Hasbro redesigns *Clue*

1987

Tonka buys Kenner Parker Toys, Inc. and the Parker Brothers brand

Glossary

app—a small, specialized program downloaded onto smartphones and other mobile devices

brand—a category of products all made by the same company

charity—an organization that helps others in need

debuted—was introduced for the first time

finances—income and expenses of a business, group, or person

Great Depression—a time in world history when many countries experienced economic crisis; the Great Depression began in 1929 and lasted through the 1930s.

headquarters—a company's main office

journalist—a person who gathers information and writes reports about the news

logo—a symbol or design that identifies a brand or product

object—the goal or purpose of a game

profit—money that is made in a business after all costs and expenses are paid

publishers—people or companies that print and sell books, magazines, music, and other works

rights—the legal ability to use a certain name or product

strategy—a plan of action designed to achieve a specific goal

tokens—pieces used to represent each player in a game

To Learn More

AT THE LIBRARY

Green, Sara. *Nerf*. Minneapolis, Minn.: Bellwether Media, 2015.

Meachen Rau, Dana. *Card Games*. Minneapolis, Minn.: Compass Point Books, 2005.

Slater, Lee. *Board Game Builder: Milton Bradley*. Minneapolis, Minn.: ABDO Publishing Company, 2016.

ON THE WEB

Learning more about Parker Brothers is as easy as 1, 2, 3.

1. Go to www.factsurfer.com.

2. Enter "Parker Brothers" into the search box.

3. Click the "Surf" button and you will see a list of related web sites.

With factsurfer.com, finding more information is just a click away.

Index